Beauty and Scripture: A Coloring Book for Adults

Floral Designs

Published by Spiritual Coloring Books

ISBN 978-0-9779149-1-3

Color exists in itself, possessing its own beauty

Henri Matisse

Therefore We do Not Lose Heart. Even Though our Outward Man is Perishing, Yet the Inward Man is being Renewed Day by Day

2 Corinthians 4:16

In the Day When I Cried Out, You Answered Me, and Made Me Bold with Strength in My Soul
Psalm 138:3

Peace I Leave
With You; My
Peace I Give You. I
Do Not Give to
You as the World
Gives. Do Not
Let Your Hearts
be Troubled and do
Not be Afraid
John 14:27

The Name of the Lord is a Strong Tower; the Righteous Run to It and are Safe
Proverbs 18:10

How Good
and Pleasant
it is When
Brothers
Live
Together in
Unity
Psalm 133:1

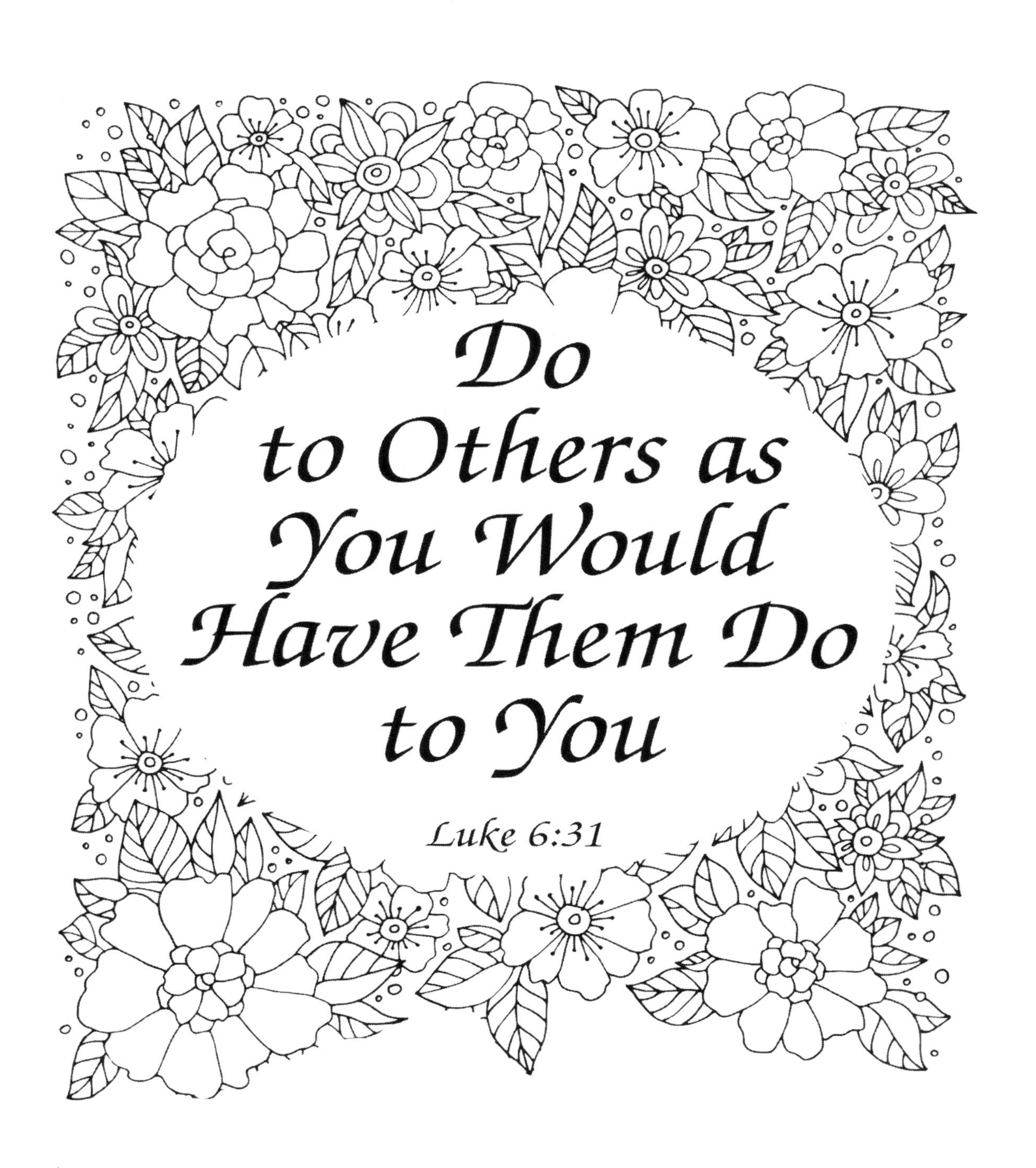
Do
to Others as
You Would
Have Them Do
to You
Luke 6:31

In All
Your
Ways
Ackno
wledge
Him,
and
He
Will
Make
Your
Paths
Straight
Proverbs 3:6

Above
All, Love
Each Other
Deeply, because
Love Covers Over
a Multitude of Sins
1 Peter 4:8

I Am the
Way and the
Truth and the Life.
No One Comes to
the Father Except
Through Me
John 14:6

Cast
All Your Anxiety
on Him
because He
Cares for You
1 Peter 5:7

Love Must
be Sincere.
Hate What
is evil; Cling
to What is
Good
Romans 12:9

Hatred
Stirs Up
Dissension,
but Love
Covers
Over All
Wrongs
Proverbs 10:12

For
God
Did Not
Send His
Son into the
World to
Condemn the
World, but to
Save the World
Through Him
John 3:17

Verily, Verily, I Say unto You, He that Believeth In Me Hath Everlasting Life.

John 6:47

Greater Love Has No One than This, that He lay Down His Life for His Friends
John 15:13

A
Friend
Loves at All
Times, and a
Brother is
Born for
Adversity
Proverbs 17:17

Whoever
Does Not
Love Does
Not Know
God, because
God is Love
1 John 4:8

When
I Am
Afraid, I
Put My
Trust in
You
Psalm 56:3

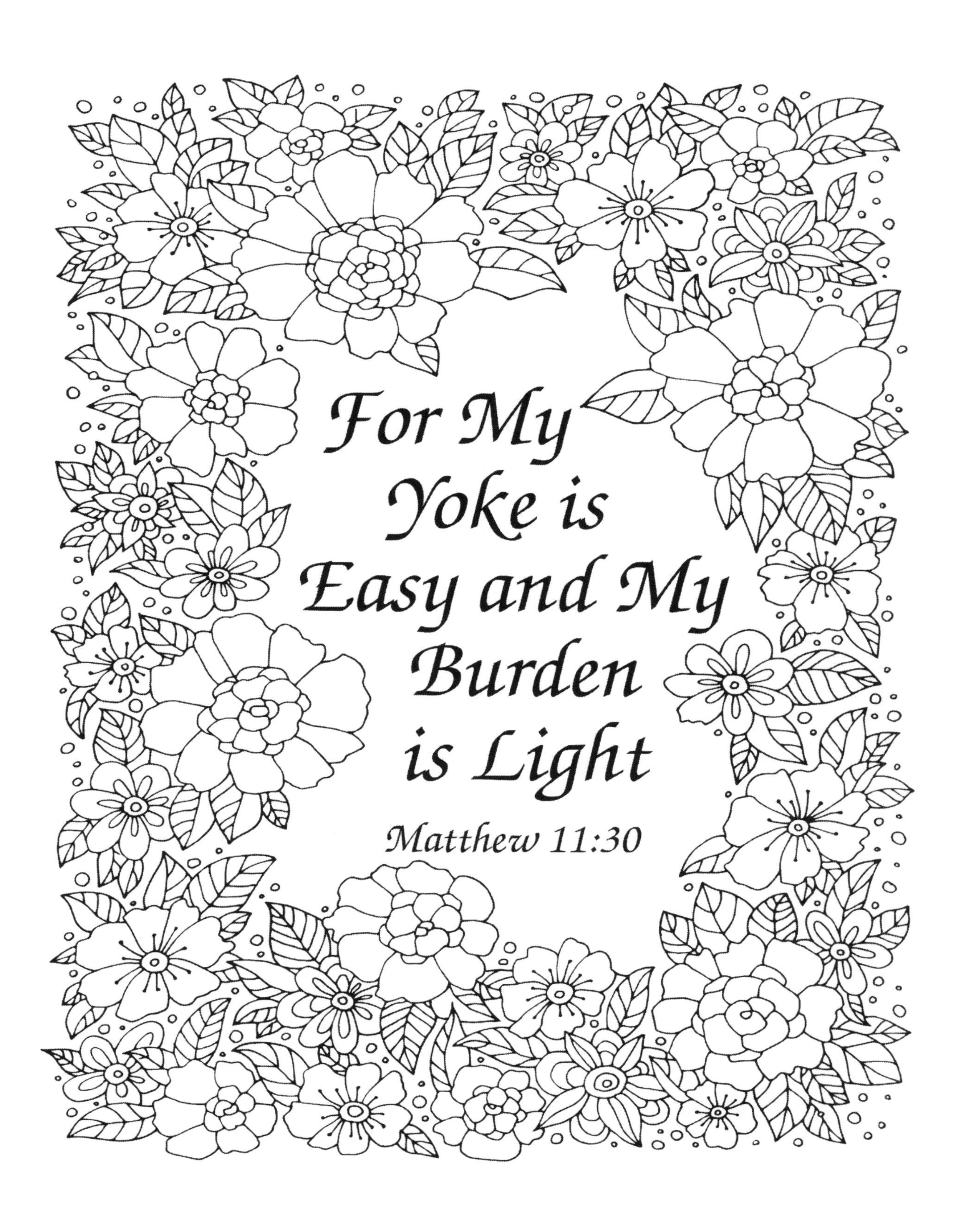
For My
Yoke is
Easy and My
Burden
is Light
Matthew 11:30

And Now
These Three
Remain: Faith,
Hope and Love.
But the
Greatest of
These is Love
1 Corinthians 13:13

Pray
Without
Ceasing
1 Thessalonians 5:17

Love Does No
Harm to its Neighbor.
Therefore Love is the
Fulfillment of the Law
Romans 13:10

O Taste and See
that the Lord
is Good:
Blessed is the
Man that
Trusteth
in Him
Psalm 34:8

With Men
This is Impossible,
but With God All
Things are
Possible
Matthew 19:26

Forever,
O Lord, Thy
Word is
Settled in
Heaven
Psalm 119:89

Look to
the Lord
and His
Strength:
Seek His
Face
Always
1 Chronicles 16:11

For All
have
Sinned
and
Fall
Short of
the Glory
of God
Romans 3:23

In the Beginning God Created the Heavens and the Earth
Genesis 1:1

Because You Know that the Testing of Your Faith Develops Perseverance
James 1:3

Blessed are the
Pure in Heart:
For They Shall
See God
Matthew 5:8

Made in the USA
San Bernardino, CA
11 December 2015